READABOUT
Clothes

© 1992 Franklin Watts

Paperback edition 1996

Franklin Watts
96 Leonard Street
London EC2A 4RH

Franklin Watts Australia
14 Mars Road
Lane Cove
NSW 2066

UK ISBN 0 7496 0859 5 (hardback)
0 7496 2640 2 (paperback)

A CIP catalogue record for this book
is available from the British Library

Editor: Ambreen Husain
Design: K and Co

Typesetting Lineage Ltd, Watford, England
Printed in Hong Kong

The Publisher and Photographer
would like to thank
Snowshoes Ski Shop, Guildford
and Bryony Harmsworth and all the children.

Additional Photographs:
Hutchison Library p.17(TR);
ZEFA pp. 7, 16(TR), 17(TL, BL, BR), 18, 24.

READABOUT
Clothes

Text: Henry Pluckrose
Photography: Chris Fairclough

W
FRANKLIN WATTS
LONDON • NEW YORK • SYDNEY

Why do we wear clothes?
When the weather is cold
we wear clothes to keep warm.
Clothes trap the heat
made by our body.
We move around in a little
parcel of our own warmth.

In hot weather we wear light-weight clothing. This helps to keep our body cool.

Clothes are made
of different materials
for different purposes.
The clothes we wear
in cold weather
are made of materials
which keep out the cold.
They also keep in the heat
made by our body.

Materials like cotton and linen are used to make light-weight clothes.

There are many different materials for clothes. Do you know what these clothes are made of?

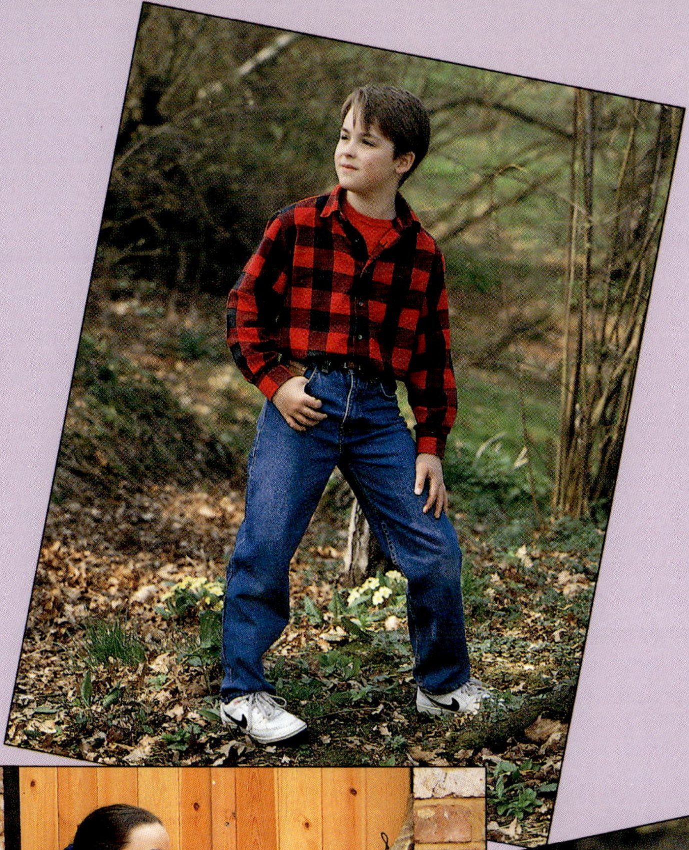
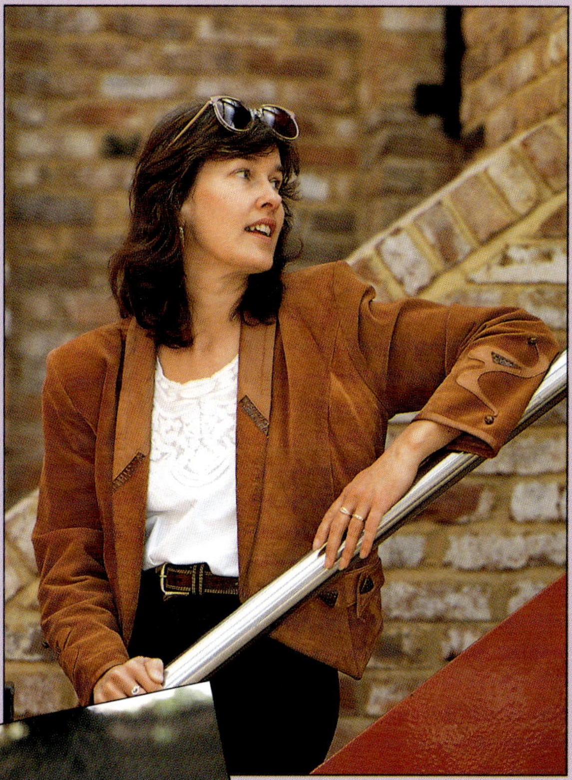
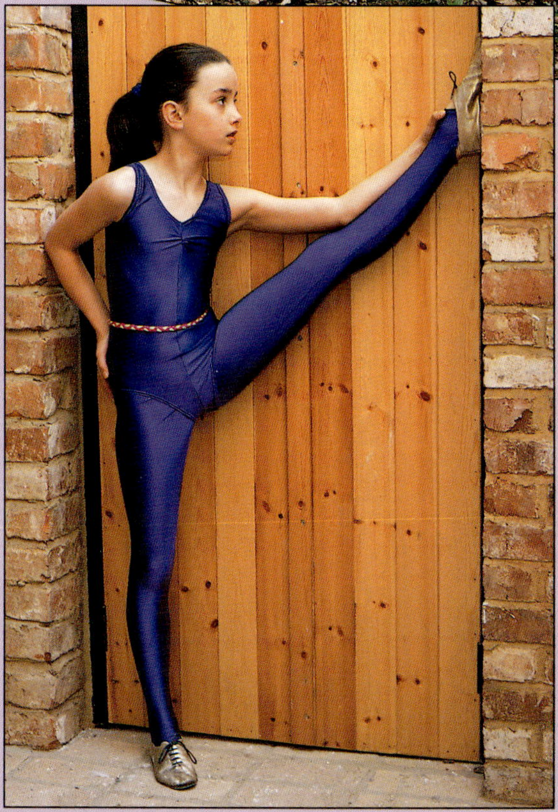
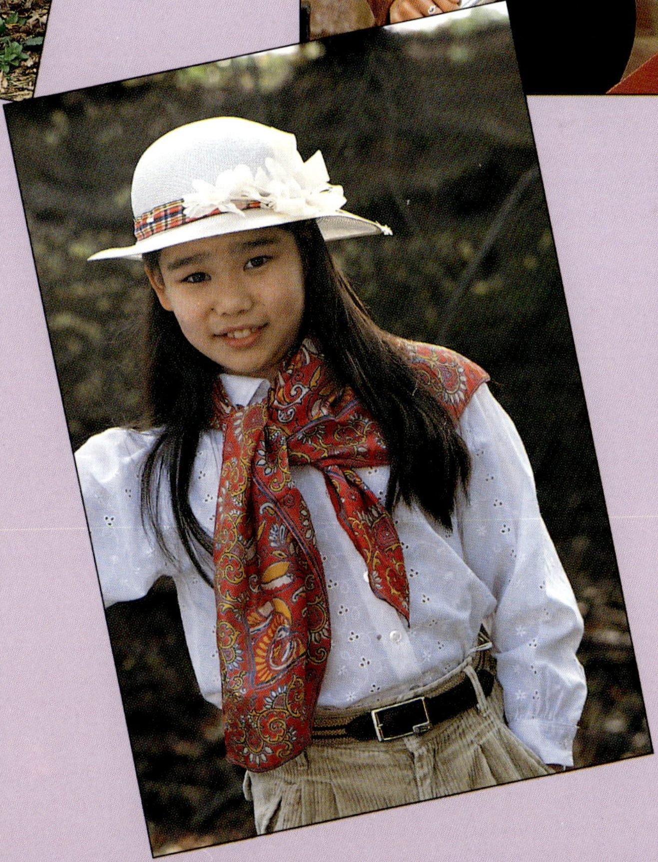

Clothes are made for almost every part of the body. There are hats...

vests, shirts, jackets and jumpers...

pants, trousers, skirts, jeans and kilts...

socks, tights, stockings, trainers, shoes and boots.

There are clothes to fit people of every shape and size.
But your clothes should fit you!

We must be sure to choose the right clothes to wear. You would not go out in your pyjamas!

Why do you think these people are wearing different kinds of clothes?

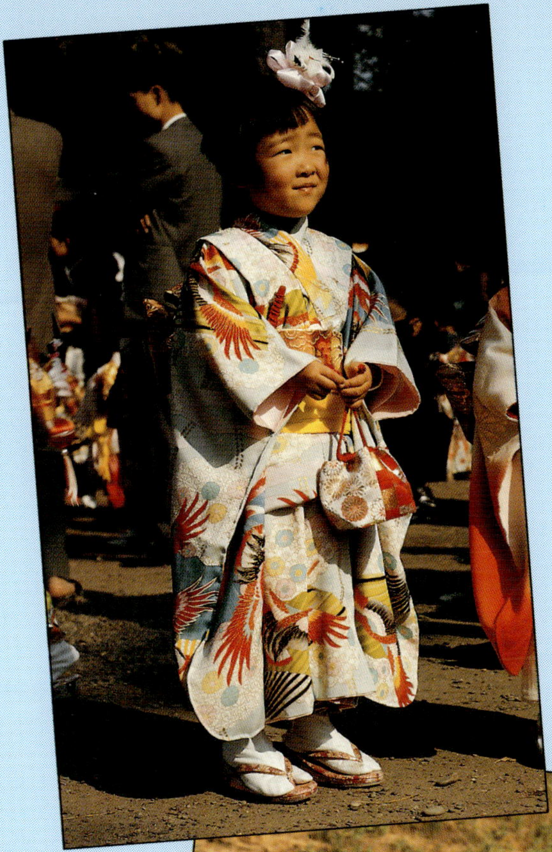
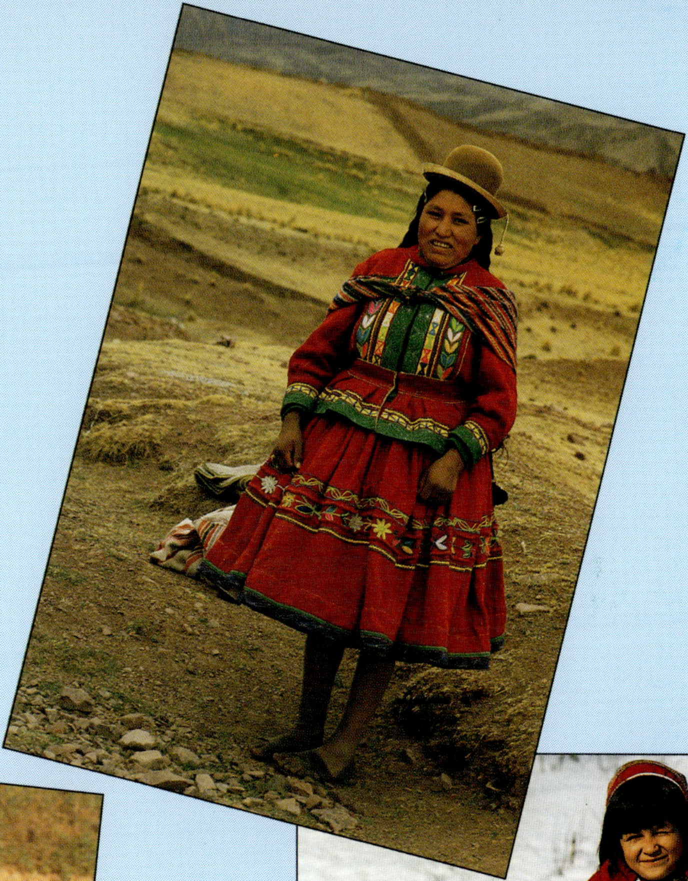
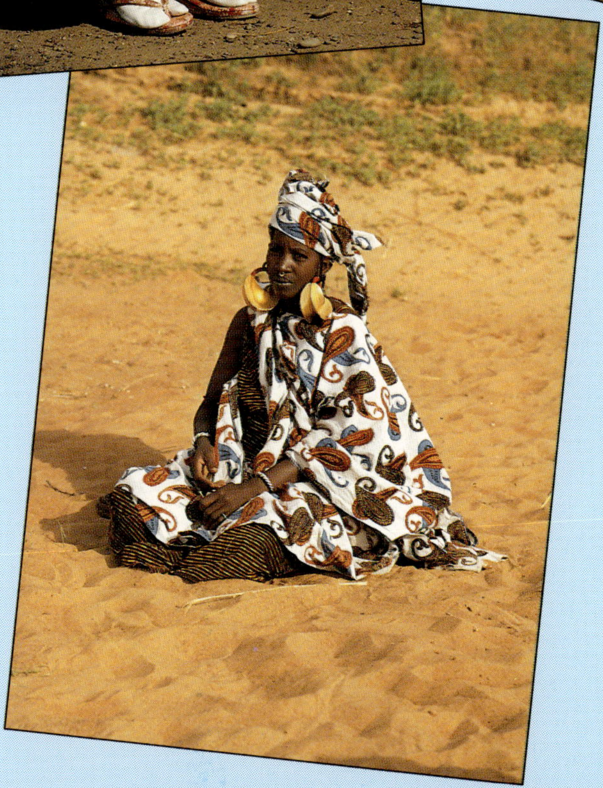
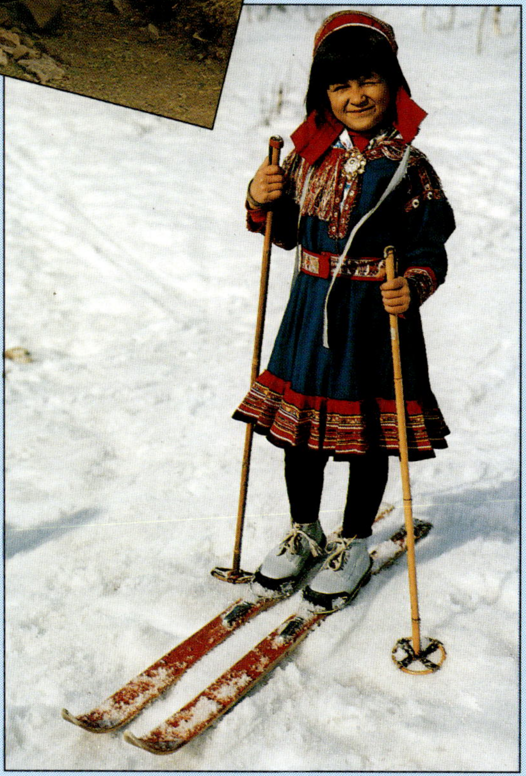

Some clothes are made
to give protection.
The diver's suit
keeps her warm
as she works beneath the sea.

These people are all wearing protective clothing. How do you think these clothes protect them?

Who might wear these for protection?

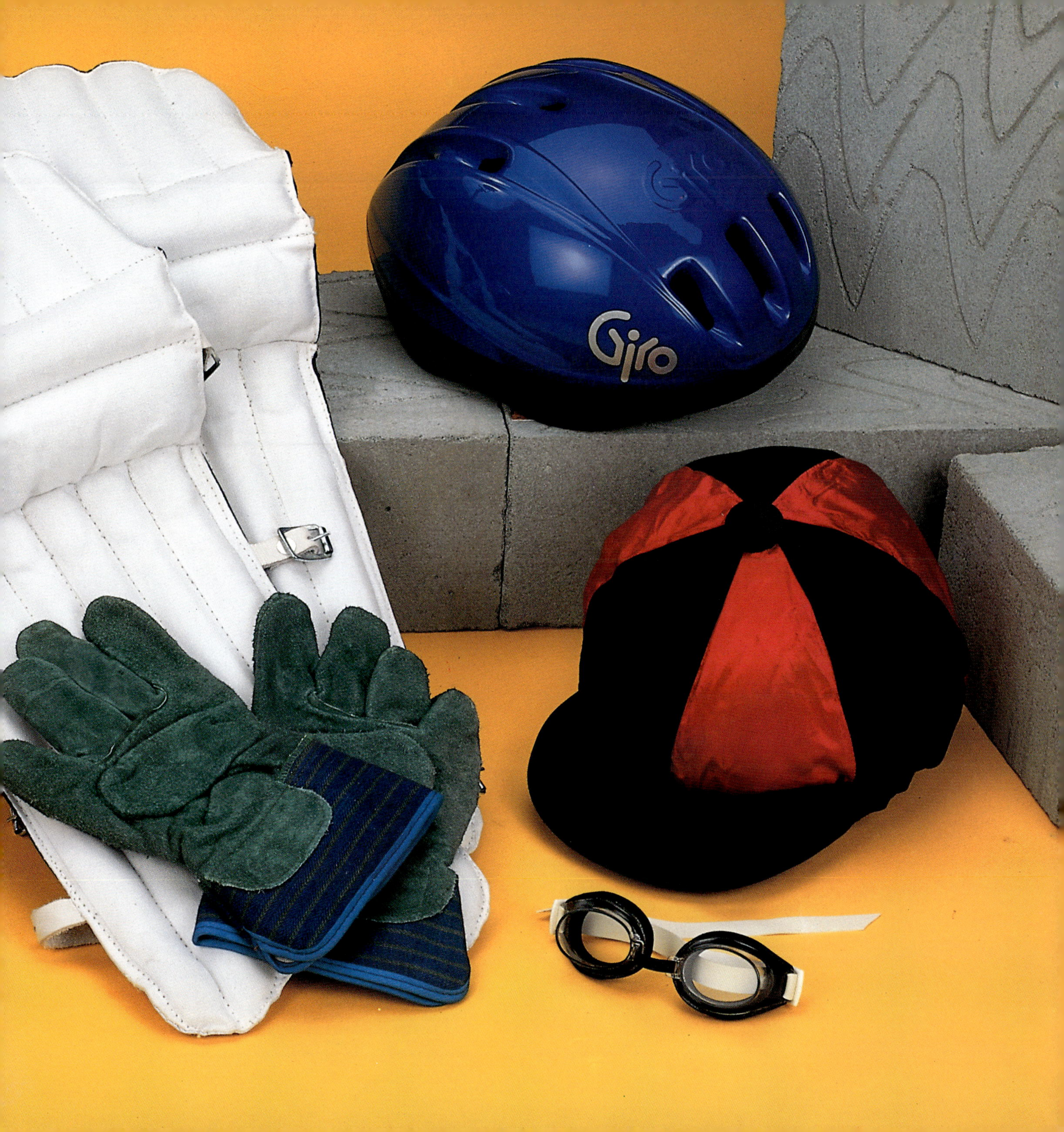
Giro

Many people wear special clothing when they are at work.

Many other workers wear uniforms too. Can you guess what work these people do?

Some people dress up for special occasions.

They change into ordinary clothes before they go home.

We wear special clothing
for sport...
to move more easily,
to show which team we are in
and for protection.
Swimmers wear costumes and caps
which will not slow them down
as they race through the water.

Shirts in team colours help you to recognize the players in your team.

The clothes people wear sometimes tell us about the things in which they believe. Clergymen wear special clothes for religious services.

Many Muslim women and girls cover their heads or wear a veil.

It would be very boring if we all wore clothes like this!

How many different kinds of clothes do you have?

About this book

All books which are specially prepared for young children are written to meet the interest of the age group at which they are directed. This may mean presenting an idea in a humorous or unconventional way so that ideas which hitherto have been grasped somewhat hazily are given sharper focus. The books in this series aim to bring into focus some of the elements of life and living which we as adults tend to take for granted.

This book develops and explores an idea using simple text and thought-provoking photographs. The words will encourage questioning and discussion – whether they are read by adult or child. Children enjoy having information books read to them just as much as stories and poetry. The younger child may ignore the written words ... pictures play an important part in learning, particularly if they encourage talk and visual discrimination.

Young children acquire much information in an incidental, almost random fashion. Indeed, they learn much just by being alive! The adult who uses books like this one needs to be sympathetic and understanding of the the young child's intellectual development. It offers a particular way of looking, an approach to questioning which will result in talk, rather than 'correct' one word answers.

Henry Pluckrose